CCSS **Genre** Narrative Nonfiction

Essential Question
How can experiencing nature change the way you think about it?

SAVE THIS SPACE!

BY MARIA GILL

D1368461

INTRODUCTION

The Grand Canyon is a spectacular place. What would it be like if the Grand Canyon were covered with signs? What if there were towns in the valleys of the Grand Canyon and if the Colorado River were filled with trash? What if the animals in the Grand Canyon were **extinct**, or had died out?

Aldo Leopold was a naturalist. He thought the Grand Canyon was a special place. He preserved the Grand Canyon and its wildlife for future generations. Verplanck Colvin thought the Adirondack Mountains in New York State were a special place. As Leopold preserved the Grand Canyon, he preserved the Adirondack Mountains and its wildlife.

This is the Grand Canyon. It is 15 miles wide at the widest point.

cliff

(t bkgd) Siede Preis/Photodisc/Getty Images, (b) Medioimages/Photodisc/Getty Images

forest

logged area

The trees on this land have been cut down by people logging the forests.

Colvin and Leopold realized that human activities such as **logging** destroyed wilderness areas. They informed people about what would happen if they didn't protect these areas.

Colvin protected the lakes and waters in the forests. Colvin made maps of the Adirondack Mountains and explored the **source**, or the origin, of the Hudson River. Leopold taught people to take care of the wildlife and the environment.

CHAPTER 1
VERPLANCK COLVIN

Verplanck Colvin was born in 1847 in Albany, New York. He became interested in nature when he was a boy. He loved to hike in the hills near his home.

When Colvin was 18, he read a book about the Adirondack Mountains. He was very excited to read about the lakes, rivers, and forests. So he decided to explore the Adirondacks.

Colvin took many trips to the Adirondacks. In 1870, he climbed Mount Seward, one of the highest mountains in the Adirondacks. He wrote about his experience:

"[There was] ... wilderness everywhere; lake on lake, river on river, mountain on mountain ..."

mountains

river

Many people enjoy hiking, fishing, and camping in the Adirondack Mountains.

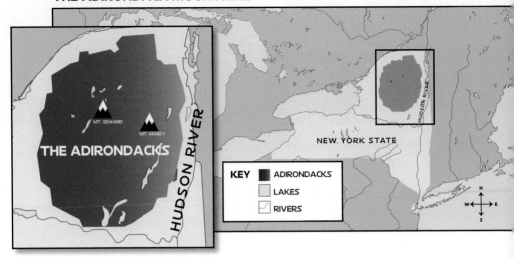

During his trips, Colvin saw the debris from logging, such as broken branches and rotting tree stumps. He realized that logging would cause terrible damage.

The sources of the Hudson River and other waterways in New York are in the Adirondack Mountains. In the spring, the snow in the mountain forests melts <u>and</u> enters the rivers and streams. This is called runoff.

The forests keep the snow from melting too fast because trees shade the snow. Colvin saw that too much logging could destroy the source of the water for the rivers and streams.

Language Detective <u>And</u> is a conjunction. What is a conjunction?

cabin

Many loggers lived in the Adirondacks while they worked.

Colvin knew that people depended on rivers and streams for water and transportation. He thought the government should protect these places.

On December 16, 1870, Colvin took ice from the Hudson River to a meeting in New York City. He made sure the ice was put into all the drinking glasses. He used the ice for emphasis. He wanted to show that everyone needed clean water. He said:

"The ice ... and the pure water ... are both fresh from ... the Hudson. We must guard our water supply ... and maintain the forests which protect the springs at the river sources ..."

At this time, there were no good maps of the Adirondack region. Colvin believed accurate maps would make it easier to protect the region from development. In 1872, the government agreed to let Colvin **survey** and map the Adirondack region.

Colvin and a team of surveyors hiked across rough land, kayaked on rivers, and climbed over sheer mountains. There were dangerous wild animals. Once, Colvin wrestled with a 7-foot-tall black bear.

To create a map, a surveyor measures and draws the surface of the land. This is called surveying.

surveyor

> "But how wild and desolate this spot! ... First seen as we then saw it, dark and dripping with the moisture of the heavens ..."
>
> Verplanck Colvin

This drawing by Colvin shows Lake Tear of the Clouds.

lake

rock

Colvin surveyed and mapped the Adirondacks for 30 years. He wrote and sketched in his journal about every lake, river, and forest he visited.

Colvin named many lakes in the Adirondacks. He followed the Hudson River and found the source, Lake Tear of the Clouds.

HOW TO MEASURE A MOUNTAIN

Colvin used a method of surveying called **triangulation**. He and his team measured a line (from point A to point B). They used a 66-foot-long chain as a measuring tape.

Then they went to the top of the mountain (point C) and used a telescope to figure out the angles between the points. Then Colvin used those angles to figure out the distances between the three points and the height of the mountain.

Colvin also **lobbied** to protect the Adirondacks. He asked the government to protect the land. He wrote editorials in newspapers to explain why it was important to protect the land. Finally in 1892, the Adirondacks became a state park. Then in 1894, the state passed a law that required the park to be "forever kept as wild." It meant the Adirondacks could not be developed.

Colvin died in 1920, but thanks to his work, people enjoy the wilderness of Adirondack Park today.

C

A

B

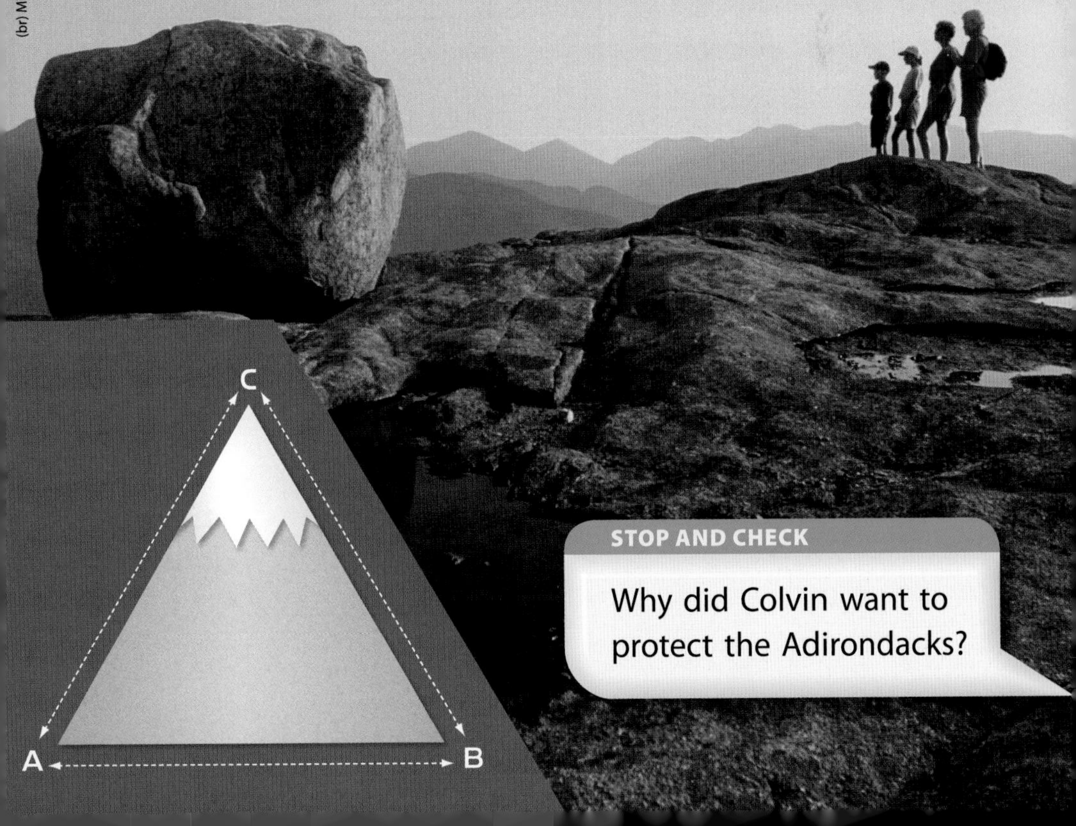

STOP AND CHECK

Why did Colvin want to protect the Adirondacks?

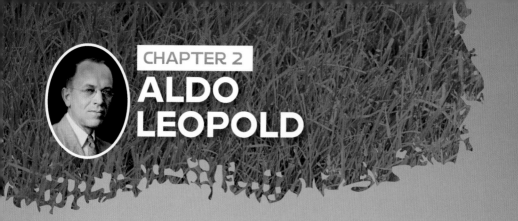

ALDO LEOPOLD

Like Colvin, Aldo Leopold loved the outdoors. Leopold was born in 1887 in Burlington, Iowa. When he was a boy, he loved to explore the woods near his home with his dog. He also liked to go hunting with his father.

In college Leopold studied forestry. After he graduated in 1909, he worked as a forest assistant in the Apache National Forest in Arizona. He enjoyed living in the mountains. In his spare time, he liked hunting **game**, such as deer and ducks. He mapped the area around Springerville, where he worked.

cloud

stream

This stream is in the Apache National Forest.

Leopold wanted to protect game animals. He believed that the forests needed to be preserved because the game animals live in forests.

Leopold also thought that people should <u>keep track of</u> the animal population. Then, they would not hunt animals that have a low population.

At that time, many people believed that game animals needed to be protected from **predators**, such as wolves, coyotes, foxes, and bears. Leopold believed that people should hunt predators to protect the game animals.

In Other Words count.
En español, *keep track of* quiere decir *vigilar*.

whiskers

Leopold hunted predators such as mountain lions. Later he worked to protect them.

paw

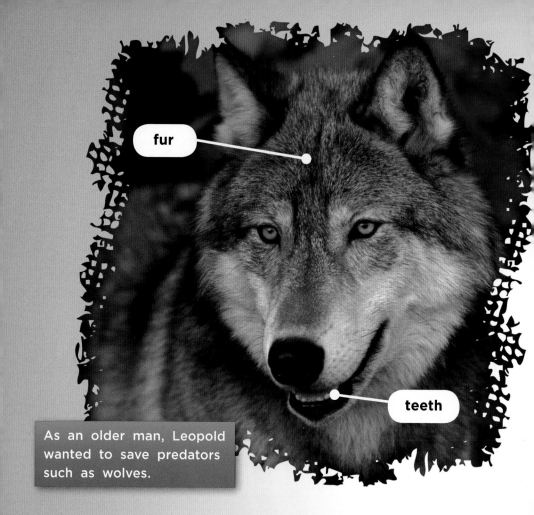

fur

teeth

As an older man, Leopold wanted to save predators such as wolves.

Later in his life, Leopold changed his ideas about predators. In the 1930s, he went on a hunting trip to Mexico. The forest in Mexico was an "unspoiled wilderness." It had been left unchanged. The predators were part of the forest **ecosystem**. The ecosystem provided a balance in the environment. As a result, the forest was healthy. Leopold realized that predators are necessary to protect the balance of the ecosystem.

Leopold had seen the effects of an unbalanced ecosystem in the forests of Wisconsin. Deer and other game animals had been protected, but predators such as wolves had been hunted. With few predators, the deer population grew very quickly. In 1942, Leopold showed people the damage deer had done to the forests. Deer had destroyed the plant life by eating all the plants within their reach. This indicated that there were too many deer in the forest.

Leopold asked the state of Wisconsin to encourage people to hunt deer. The deer population decreased. He also asked people to stop hunting wolves. The wolf population increased. People realized that Leopold's plan created a balanced ecosystem.

deer

"You cannot love game and hate predators ... The land is one organism."

Aldo Leopold

Deer can do a lot of damage to a forest if the population is not controlled.

In addition to protecting wildlife, Leopold also worked to protect the landscape. In 1915, Leopold went to the Grand Canyon, and he was shocked by the state of it. There were new roads, hotels, and stores. He saw trash on the trails, <u>and</u> sewage ran into the river. Leopold knew these things were bad for the wildlife.

Leopold created a plan to protect the wildlife and the landscape of the Grand Canyon. In 1919, the Grand Canyon was made a national park.

Language Detective

<u>And</u> is a conjunction. Find another conjunction on page 13.

David Forman/Image Source

canyon

Millions of tourists visit the Grand Canyon each year. So, there are laws to protect the park from pollution and damage.

The Gila National Forest has spectacular scenery.

Leopold also worked to preserve 750,000 acres in the Gila National Forest in New Mexico. In 1924, the forest became the first protected wilderness area in the world. This means that people cannot change the area in any way. For example, people cannot build roads in the forest.

Leopold died in 1948. Sixteen years later, in 1964, the federal government passed the Wilderness Act. The new law included many of Leopold's ideas. It established the National Wilderness Preservation System. This system protects more than 500 wilderness areas in 44 states. The United States still has places that are "natural, wild, and free" because of Aldo Leopold's work.

Aldo Leopold walks with his dog.

STOP AND CHECK

Why did Leopold want to protect predators?

CONCLUSION

People enjoy wilderness areas today because of the work of people such as Verplanck Colvin and Aldo Leopold.

Colvin wanted to protect forests so that there would be clean drinking water. He located the sources of rivers, created maps, and surveyed the mountains in the Adirondacks.

EXTINCT BIRDS

These birds have all become extinct in North America since the 1850s.

Carolina parakeet

passenger pigeon

Labrador duck

Aldo Leopold taught people to take care of the environment. We can help by:

- using fewer **natural resources** so there is less waste;

- growing plants at home;

- growing plants or trees that attract birds;

- learning about nature and recording what we find out in a journal.

We should enjoy nature, but when we take a walk in a park or forest, we should be careful to preserve it.

backpack

These hikers are enjoying the view.

hiker

Jeremy Woodhouse/Blend Images LLC

Respond to Reading

Summarize

Use important details from *Save This Space!* to summarize the text. Your graphic organizer may help you.

Cause → Effect		
	→	
	→	
	→	
	→	

Text Evidence

1. What text features help you identify this text as an example of narrative nonfiction? **GENRE**

2. Reread page 5. What caused Colvin to realize that the wilderness areas had to be protected? **CAUSE AND EFFECT**

3. Find the word *state* on page 13. What is the meaning of the word? Use context clues to help you. What is the meaning of the word *state* on page 14? **HOMOGRAPHS**

4. In Chapter 2, Leopold changes his mind about hunting predators. Write about what caused him to change his mind. **WRITE ABOUT READING**

Compare Texts

Read about how the Lewis and Clark expedition changed the way people thought about nature.

The Journey of Lewis and Clark

Lewis

Clark

In 1804, Meriwether Lewis and William Clark <u>set out</u> on an **expedition** to what would later become the northwestern United States. President Thomas Jefferson instructed them to look for a water route from Ohio to the Pacific Ocean.

Lewis and Clark saw many amazing sights. They saw plants and animals that they had never seen before. They drew maps of their journey and recorded their experiences in journals. On May 5, 1805, Lewis wrote about two species of wolves that are now extinct. One species was small and lived in burrows on the plains. The other species was bigger. It lived in the woods and on the plains, but it did not dig burrows.

> **In Other Words** went. En español, *set out* quiere decir *salir*.

Wild Adventures

Native Americans told them about bears. The Native Americans said the bears were very big and hard to kill. The first bears that Lewis and Clark saw were small. Lewis wrote about bears:

"[They] ... are [not] as formidable or dangerous as they have been represented." April 29, 1805

Lewis soon changed his mind. On June 14, 1805, he was walking alone along the Missouri River. He was carrying a spear. Suddenly he saw a grizzly bear. It was coming toward Lewis. He described what happened next in his journal.

"I ran about 80 yards and found he gained on me fast ..."

Lewis ran into the river and aimed the spear at the bear. The bear turned around and went off in the other direction. After this encounter, Lewis told everyone not to travel alone.

Grizzly bears, like the one that charged at Lewis, can weigh more than 800 pounds.

Magnificent Landscapes

As they traveled, Lewis and Clark observed spectacular scenes. In this journal entry, Lewis describes the Multnomah Falls in Oregon.

"We passed several beautiful cascades which fell from a great height over the stupendous rocks, and the most remarkable of these cascades falls about 300 feet ... several small streams fall from a much greater height, and in their descent become a perfect mist ..."
April 9, 1806

Clarkia pulchella

By the end of their expedition, Lewis and Clark had collected many **specimens** of animals and unusual plants. Scientists studied their journals and specimens for many years.

Lewis collected this specimen of a plant. The name of the plant is ragged robin, or *Clarkia pulchella*.

Make Connections

How did Lewis and Clark change the way people thought about nature? **ESSENTIAL QUESTION**

How do the early explorers in this book help you to understand why it's important to value and conserve the wilderness? **TEXT TO TEXT**

Glossary

ecosystem all the living things, such as plants and animals, and nonliving things, such as soil, water, and sunlight, that exist in one place or environment and how these things interact *(page 12)*

expedition journey or trip taken for a specific purpose *(page 19)*

extinct died out or no longer in existence (page 2)

game wild animals or birds that people hunt for sport or for food *(page 10)*

lobbied tried to influence public officials *(page 9)*

logging cutting down trees to use the wood for buildings or other products *(page 3)*

natural resources materials such as coal, trees, minerals, and water that are found in nature and can be used by people *(page 17)*

predators animals that hunt and eat other animals *(page 11)*

source where a river begins *(page 3)*

specimens plants or animals collected as an example of that species *(page 21)*

survey find out the size, shape, and position of an area of land *(page 7)*

triangulation a method used to find heights or distances by using known lengths and the angles of triangles *(page 8)*

Index

Focus on
Social Studies

Purpose To understand the importance of the wilderness

What to Do

Step 1 ▶ Work with a partner or in a group. Find out what kind of wilderness existed in your area 150 years ago. Use information from the local city or town offices, museum, or historical society.

Step 2 ▶ Create a map or drawing that shows what the area was like 150 years ago. For example, make a map showing forests that existed in the area or drawings of animals or plants that lived in the area.

Step 3 ▶ Identify the things on the map or drawing that have changed in the last 150 years. For example, show an area of forest that has changed into a neighborhood or a species of animal that no longer lives in the area.

Step 4 ▶ Select one item from your map or drawing and write sentences to describe the change.